Inquisitive Ellis asks:

# "Where is my Funny Bone?"

*Julianne Wells*
Julianne Wells, Author
Fran Hughes, Illustrator

All rights reserved

Text Copyright @ 2015

Illustrations copyright @ Fran Hughes, 2015

The right of Julianne Wells and identified as the author of this work and illustrator, Fran Hughes respectively has been asserted by them in accordance with the Copyright, Designs and Patents Act, 1988.

This book is sold subject to the condition that it shall not, by way of trade or otherwise be lent, resold, hired out, or otherwise circulated without the publisher's prior consent in any form of binding or cover other than that which it is published and without a similar condition, including this condition, being imposed upon the subsequent purchaser.

ISBN-13: 978-1499722666

www.inquisitiveellis.com

## DEDICATION

To my inquisitive granddaughter, Iris, and her little brother, Porter; proof that children, grandchildren and books achieve your immortality.

# TABLE OF CONTENTS

Foreword p. 1

"Where is my Funny Bone?" p. 2

Scientific Explanation p. 34

Anatomy of the Elbow drawing p. 35

Bone Facts p. 36

Etymology of the Phrase p. 37

About the Inquisitive Ellis Construction Team p. 38

# FOREWORD

Ellis can only understand the literal meaning of phrases and words. His questions and his answers come to life in the following books:

*Inquisitive Ellis asks: "There's a Frog in my Throat?"*

*Inquisitive Ellis asks: "Where is my Funny Bone?"*

Ellis is having a snack in the kitchen after school while the TV is on in the family room. Eleanor, his sister, is usually watching some dance show, but today Eleanor is not in the room. Ellis looks out the window to see his Mom in the yard walking Gus, their dog. Gus is a Westie the family named after Ellis' grandfather, Augustus. "Granddad loved dogs. I love dogs, too," Ellis thinks to himself. "Mom thinks Gus is smelly sometimes, especially when he's wet."

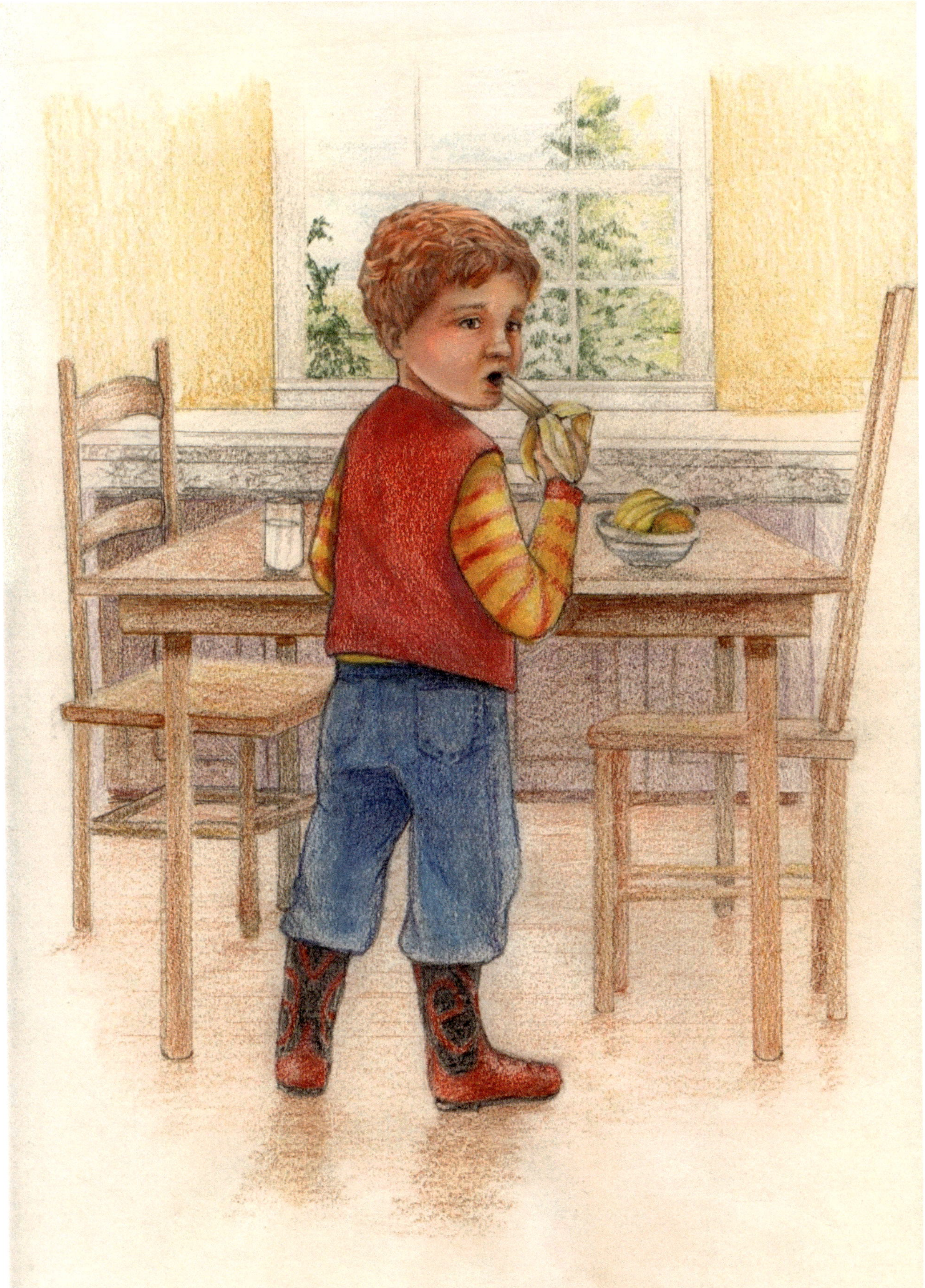

Ellis hears a person on the TV in the family room say, "There are 206 bones in your body if you don't include the funny bone (Ha! Ha! Ha!)" laughs the announcer on TV. "What a great bone that is because you can't break it!" He laughs again with the audience. Confused, Ellis rushes to the family room with his banana in his hand to see the television but a commercial is on instead.

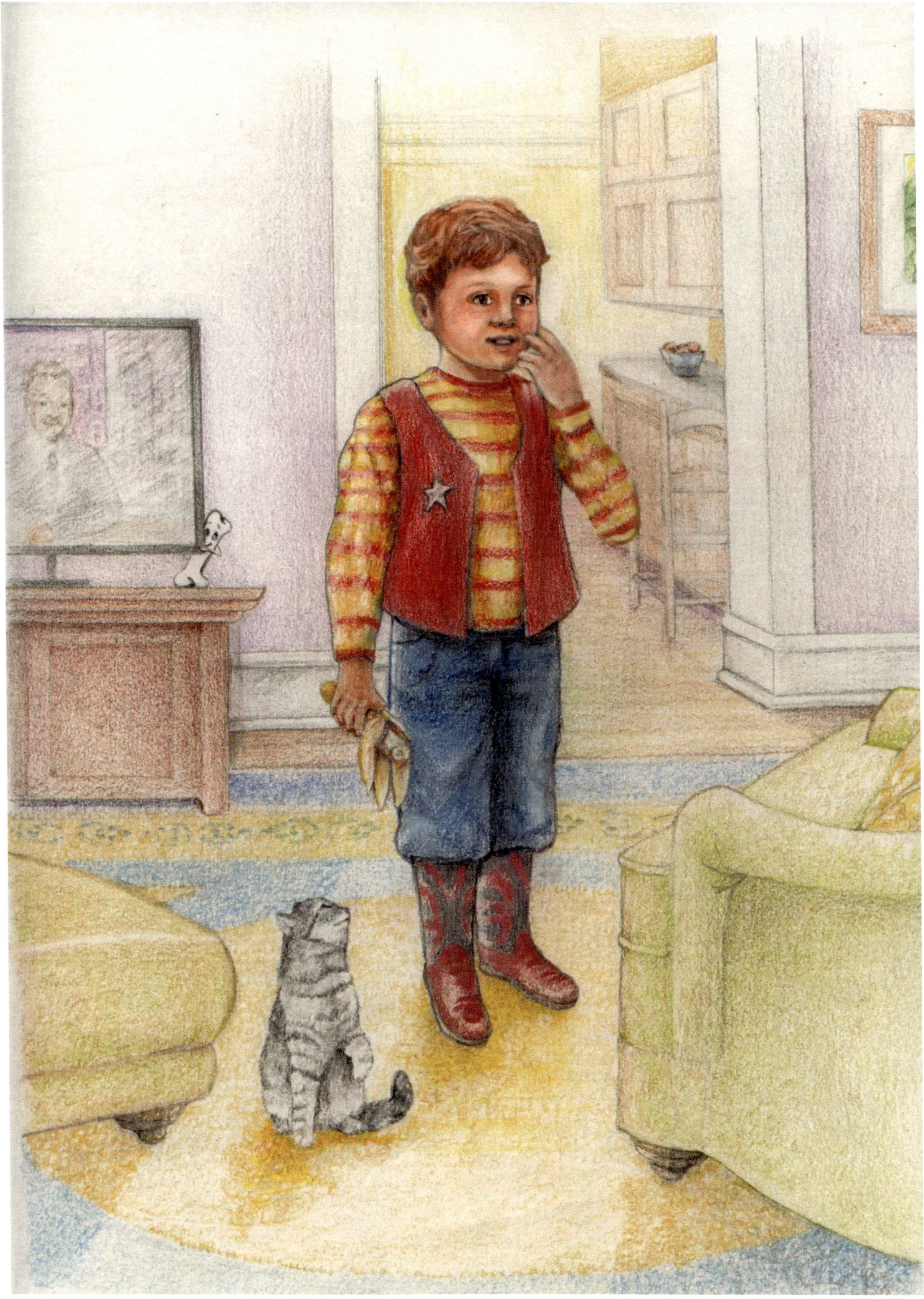

"A funny bone? Is that what he said? What's a funny bone?" Ellis asks without anyone in the room. He stares at the TV waiting for an answer. The television person is back on and is talking about a dance step. "Yuck!" thinks Ellis, sitting down on the couch. "I wanted to hear about the funny bone, not people dancing! So, I wonder where the funny bone is in my body. 206 bones! That's a lot! Hmm! I know, I'll ask Eleanor!"

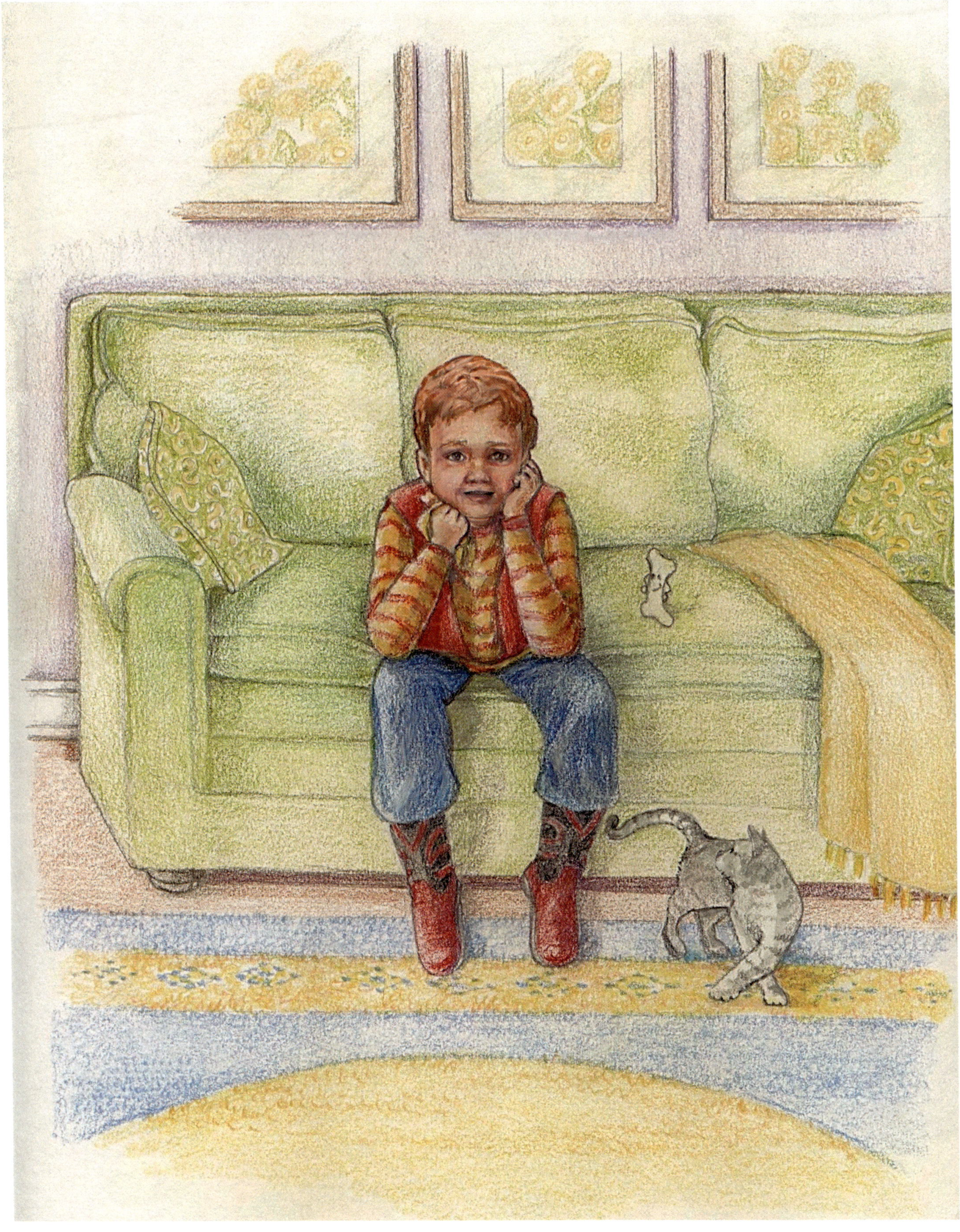

"HEY! ELEANOR!!! EL-LEA-NOR!!!!!" yells Ellis, louder and louder as he is running down the hall looking for his sister. She is in her bedroom doing homework.

"Eleanor," Ellis interrupts his sister who is reading, "Do I have a funny bone? The man on TV said there are 206 bones in the body and a funny bone. Do I have a funny bone? Do you have a funny bone? Does Gus have a funny bone? I've never seen a dog laugh. Do dogs laugh? Does Mom have..."

"Wait. What?" Eleanor says while putting her book down. "A funny bone?" Eleanor repeats, "A funny bone? Why, yes, everyone has a funny bone," Eleanor explains.

"Does it make you funny?" asks Ellis with a big grin.

"It sure does!" answers Eleanor, giggling. "It makes you feel real funny."

9

Thinking that was enough of an explanation, Eleanor runs off to answer the phone she left in her back pack on the kitchen table.

But for Ellis, the search for his funny bone has just begun.

"If everybody has a funny bone," thinks Ellis, "where is my funny bone?"

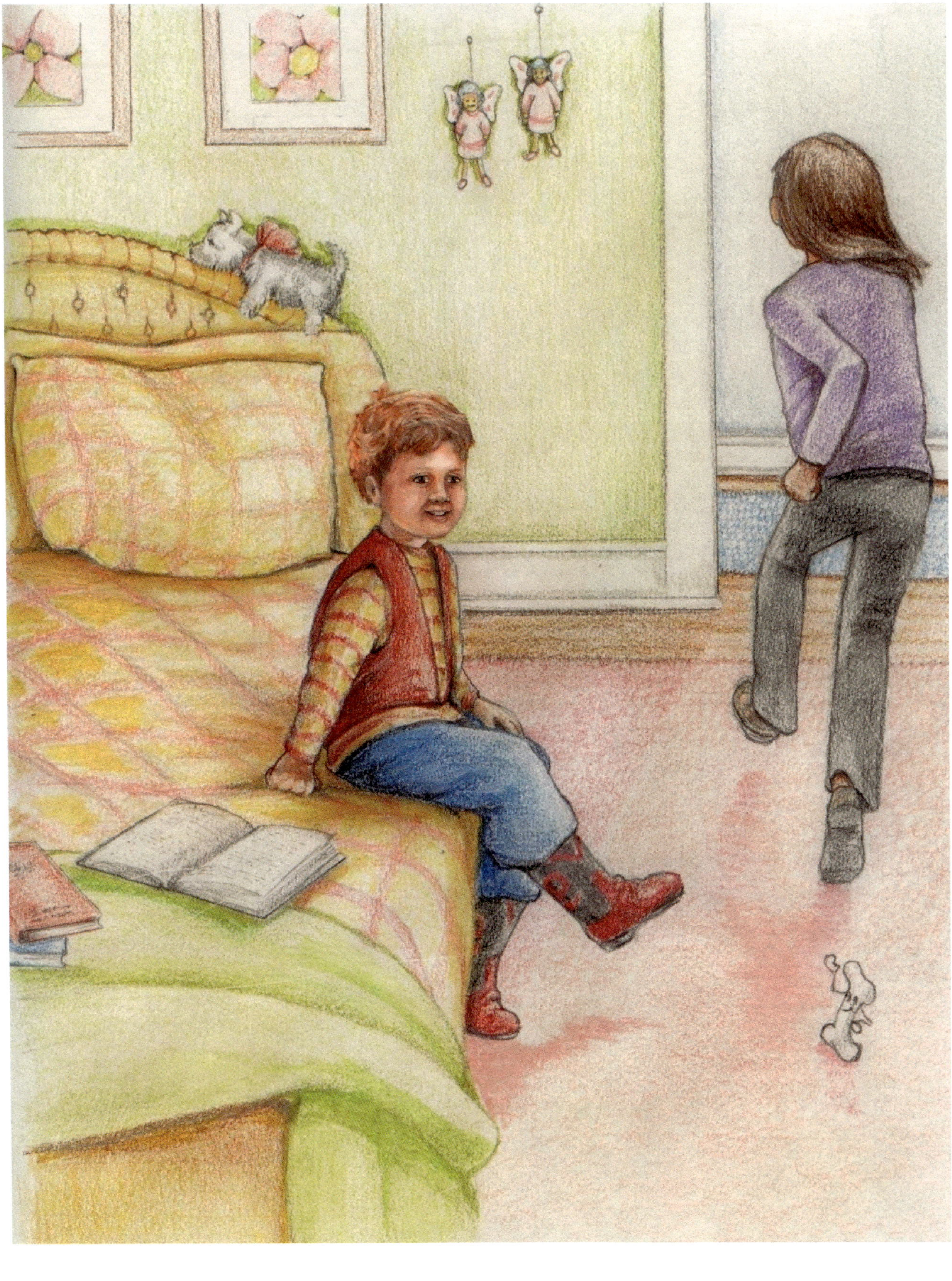

Ellis walks to the park so he can think about this important question. Ellis goes to the park almost every day except when it is raining. He can walk through the gate in his back yard to get to the park.

He sees two mothers from his neighborhood sitting on a bench talking and watching their children play on the swings. One of the mothers starts to laugh and holds her stomach.

"So your funny bone must be in your stomach," thinks Ellis. "Hmm!!"

Ellis feels his stomach and says to himself, "I don't feel any bones in my stomach."

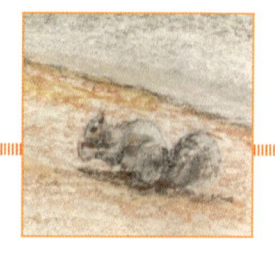

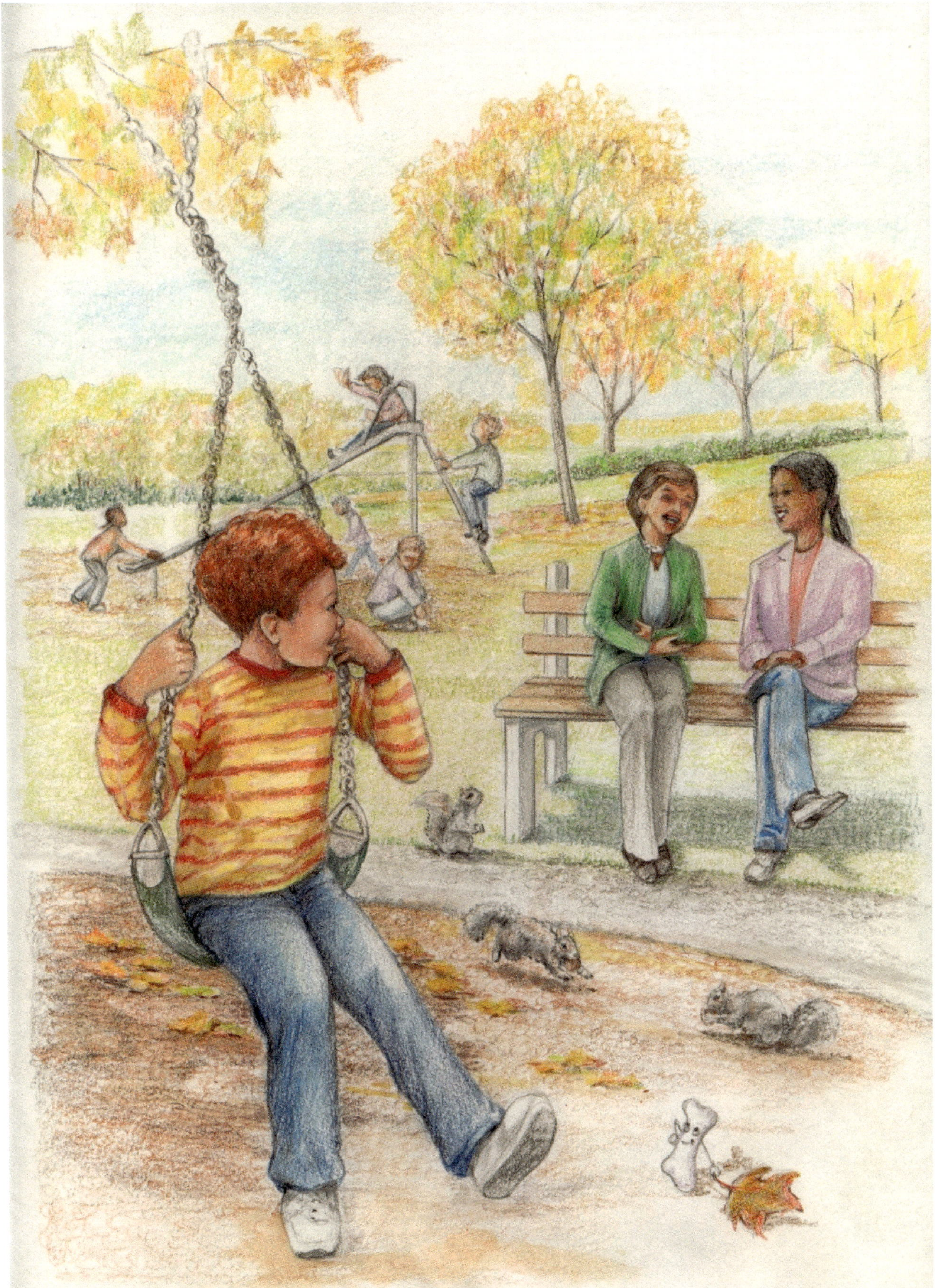

Ellis continues to walk looking for people who are laughing.

He sees a boy telling his father a story.

Ellis watches as the father throws his head back and releases a loud laugh.

"The funny bone must be in the neck," thinks Ellis. He feels his neck. "There are lots of bones in my neck, but which one is it?"

(There are actually thirty three bones in your neck.)

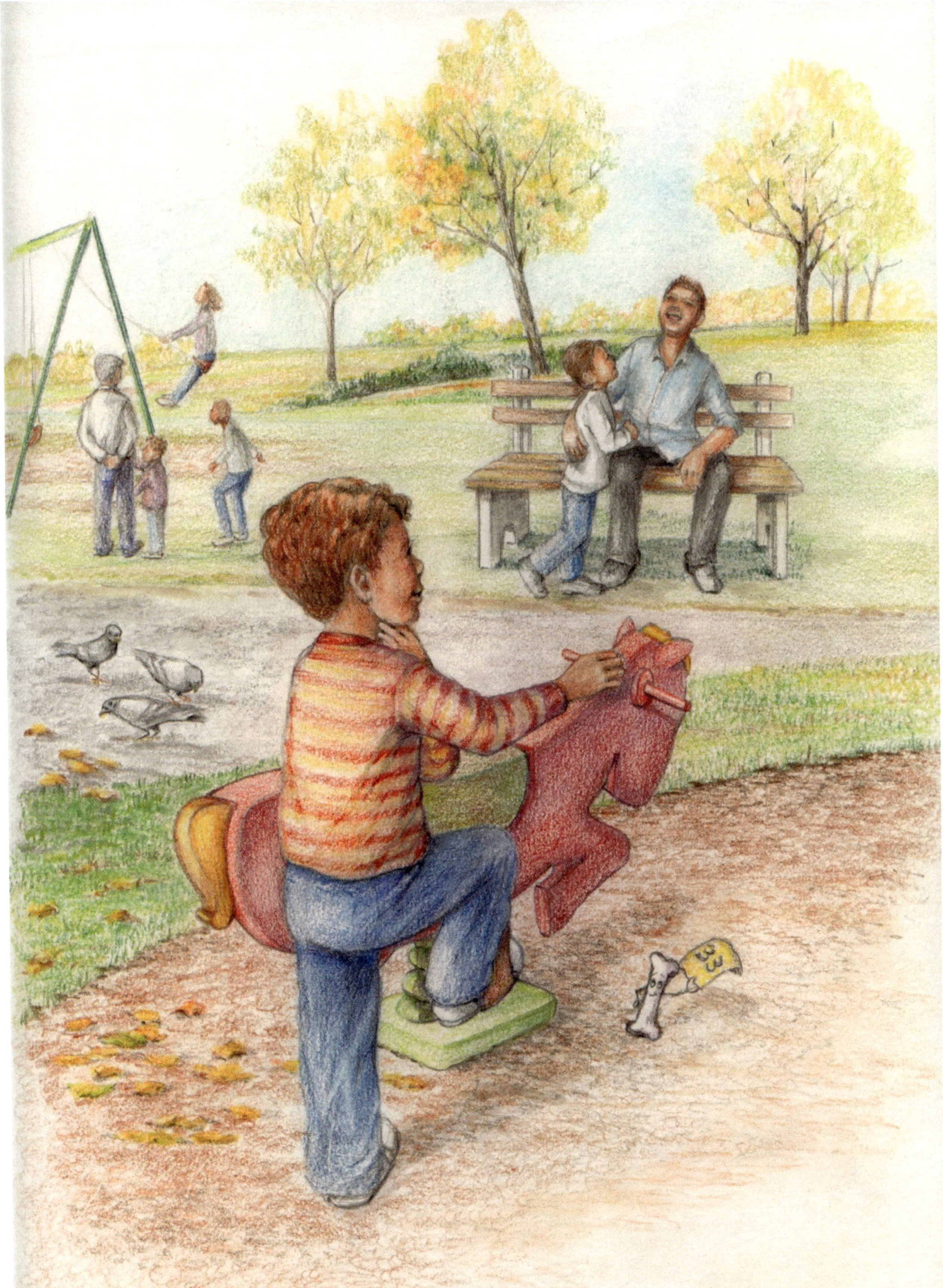

As Ellis is walking out of the park, he overhears a person say, "Oh! That was a good one, George!" The man slaps his leg and continues to laugh. "Ha! Ha! Ha! A really good one!"

"Is the funny bone in the leg?" Ellis asks himself. "That's a really big bone. Is that why adults are funnier because they have longer legs than kids? Ahhh!" Ellis moans, frustrated.

Not finding an answer, Ellis starts for home.

(That long bone is called the Femur bone.)

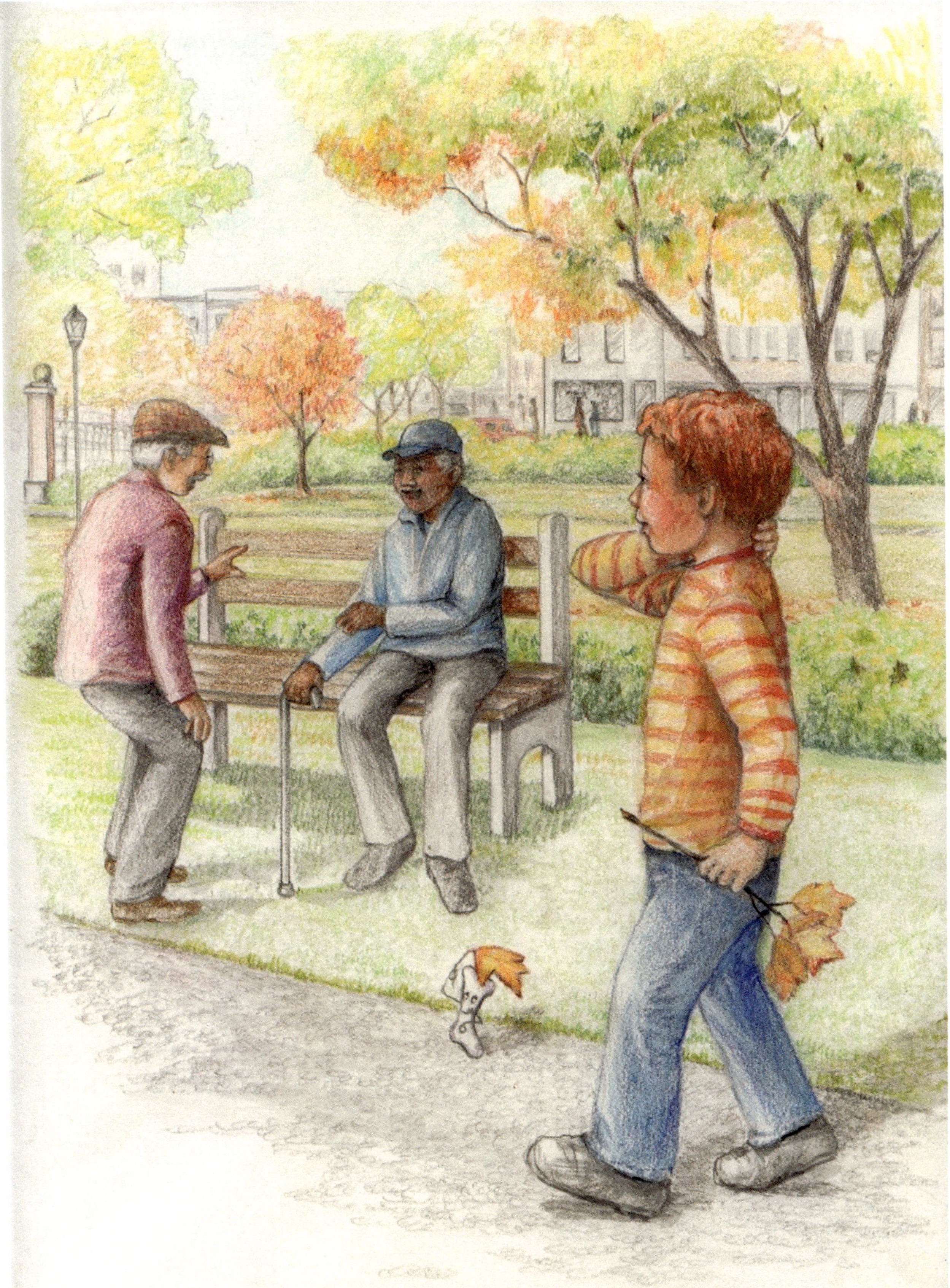

Ellis pushes open the back door to his house and the screen door slams behind him. He finds his Mom in the kitchen making meatloaf for dinner. Eleanor is stirring the meat and other ingredients together.

"Hello Ellis! Did you have fun at the park?" asks his Mom.

"Yeah, I guess so," he answers, glumly.

"Hi Ellis," Eleanor says. "I was just telling Mom a joke. See if you can get it."

"So Mom, what do you get when you mix a buffalo and a loaf of bread?"

"I don't know," giggles Mom.

"A buff-a-loaf," says Eleanor, laughing.

Mom chuckles and puts her hand over her mouth and then laughs louder.

Ellis thinks to himself, "The funny bone must be on the mouth, but there are no bones on my mouth, just squishy lips." Ellis touches his mouth, just to be sure, but only feels hard teeth.

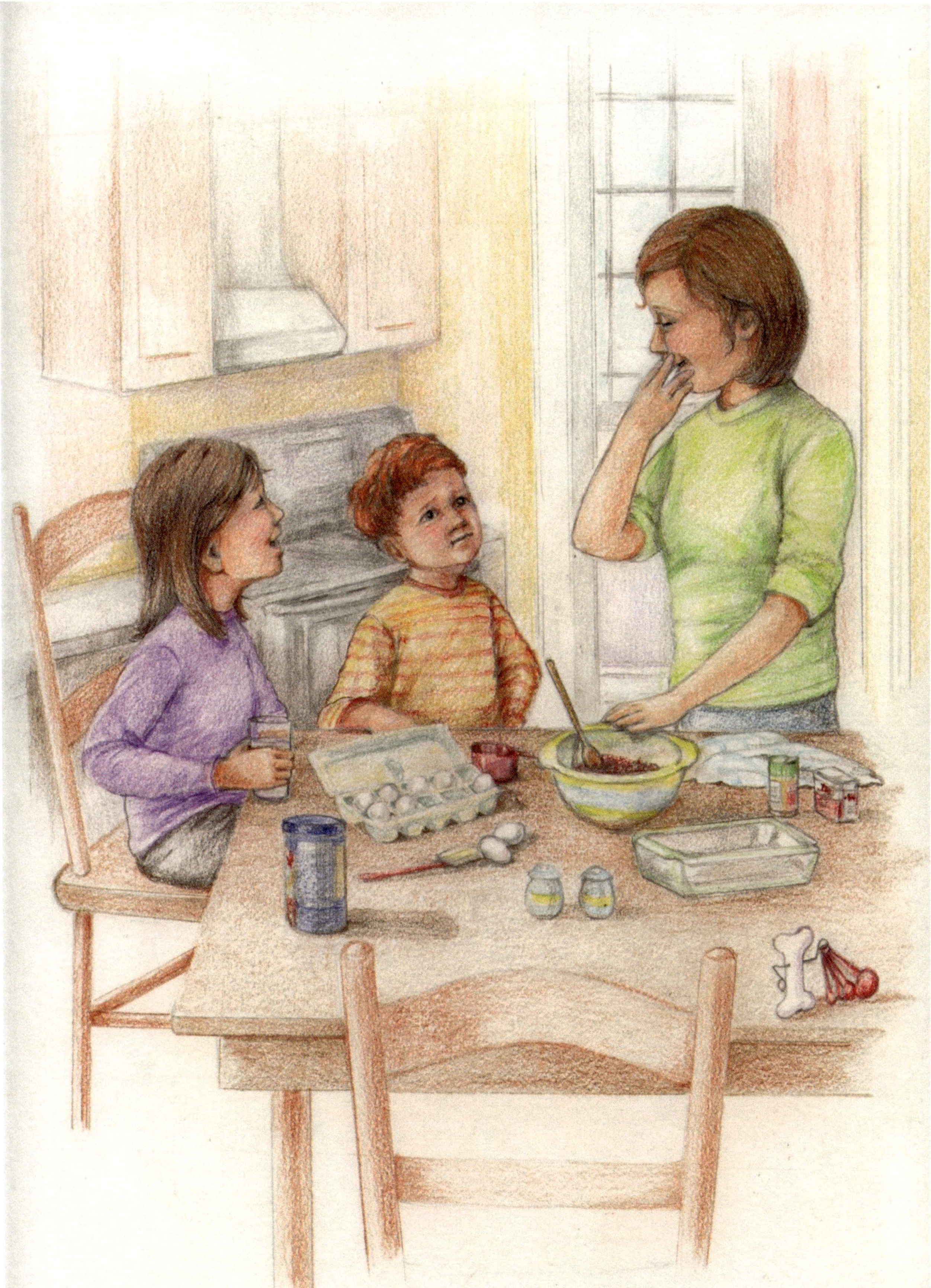

Mom turns around to look at Ellis when she didn't hear him laughing at Eleanor's joke.

"What is it, Ellis? Don't you get the joke? Here, I'll explain it to you."

"Mom!" Ellis interrupts, "Do I have a funny bone?"

"What? Well, of course you do!" Mom replies.

"Well, where is it?" Ellis asks, frustrated.

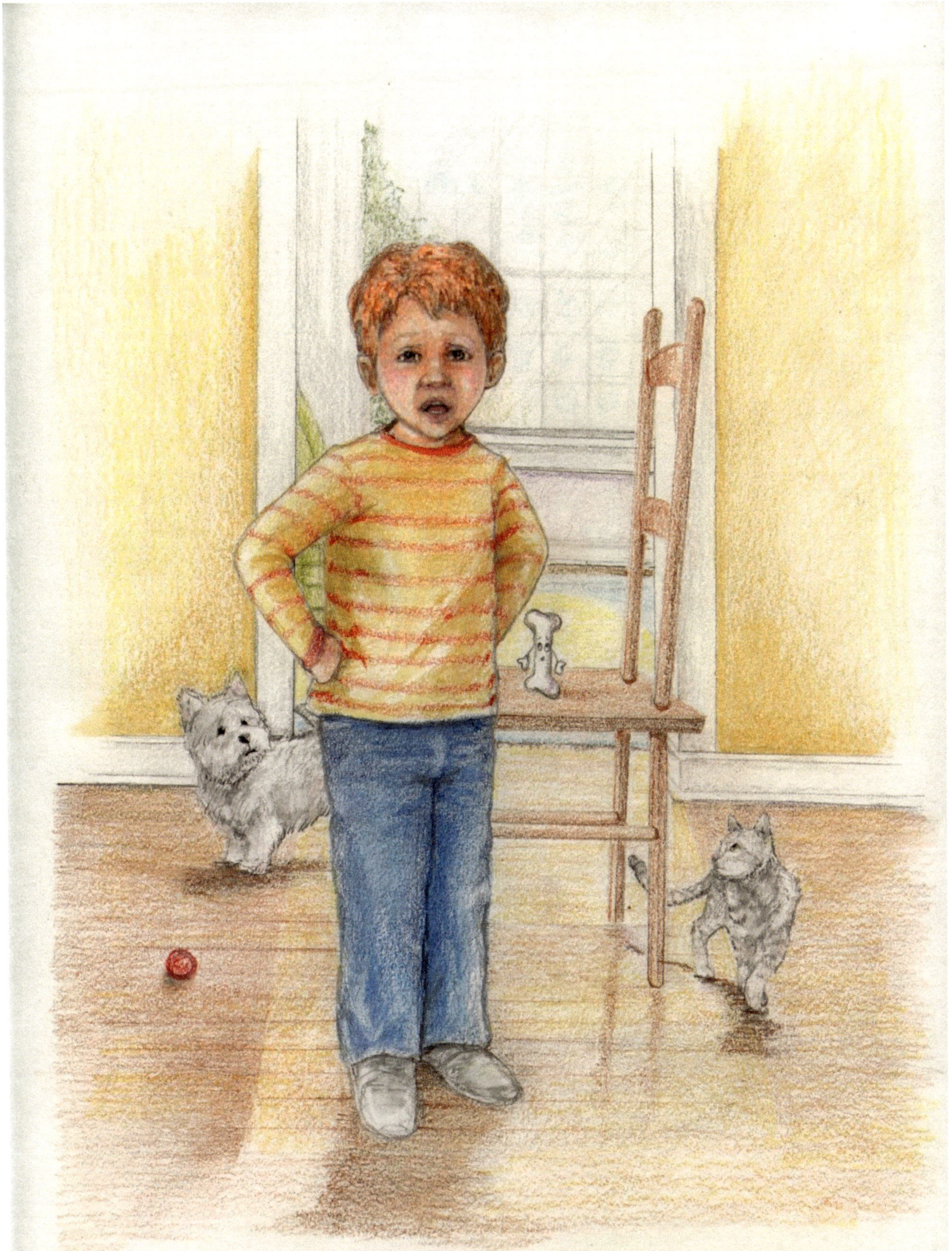

Confused and waiting for an answer, Ellis stares at his mother.

While his mother thinks of an answer, Ellis begins to speak. "Is my funny bone in my stomach because I don't feel any bones in my stomach? Is my funny bone in my neck because there are lots of bones in my neck? Is my funny bone in my leg? That's a really big bone in my leg. Is my funny bone in my mouth? WHERE IS MY FUNNY BONE?"

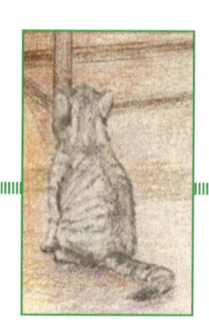

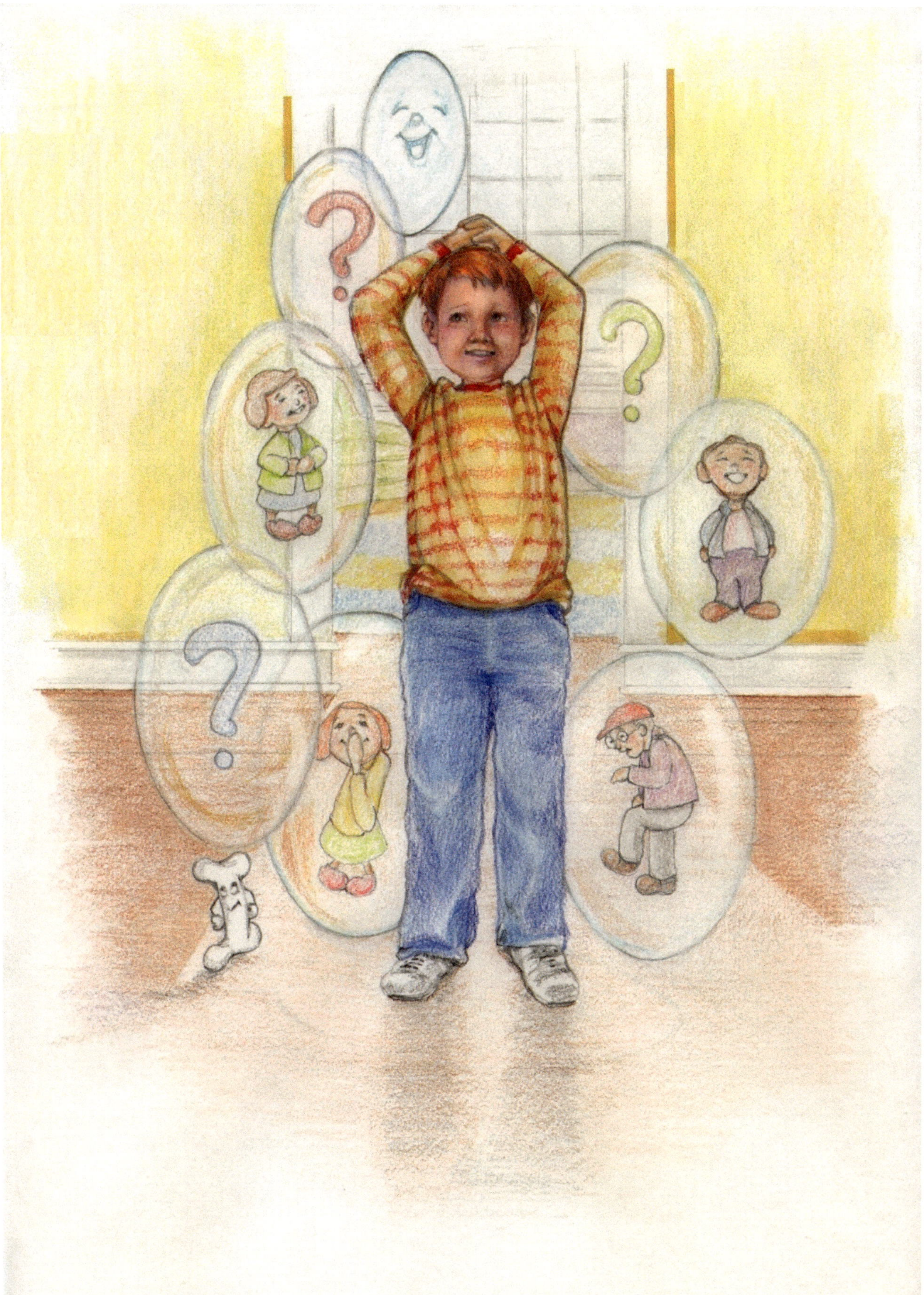

Ellis' Mom pauses and slowly and quietly says, almost whispering, "It's in your elbow." Ellis' Mom watches his face for a reaction.

"My elbow? MY ELBOW?" Ellis repeats in disbelief and a little louder. "How can my funny bone be in my elbow?" Ellis tries poking his elbow with his finger like he's pushing a button, but it is not making him laugh. He tries squishing his elbow like he is squeezing a lemon for lemonade, but that doesn't make him laugh, either.

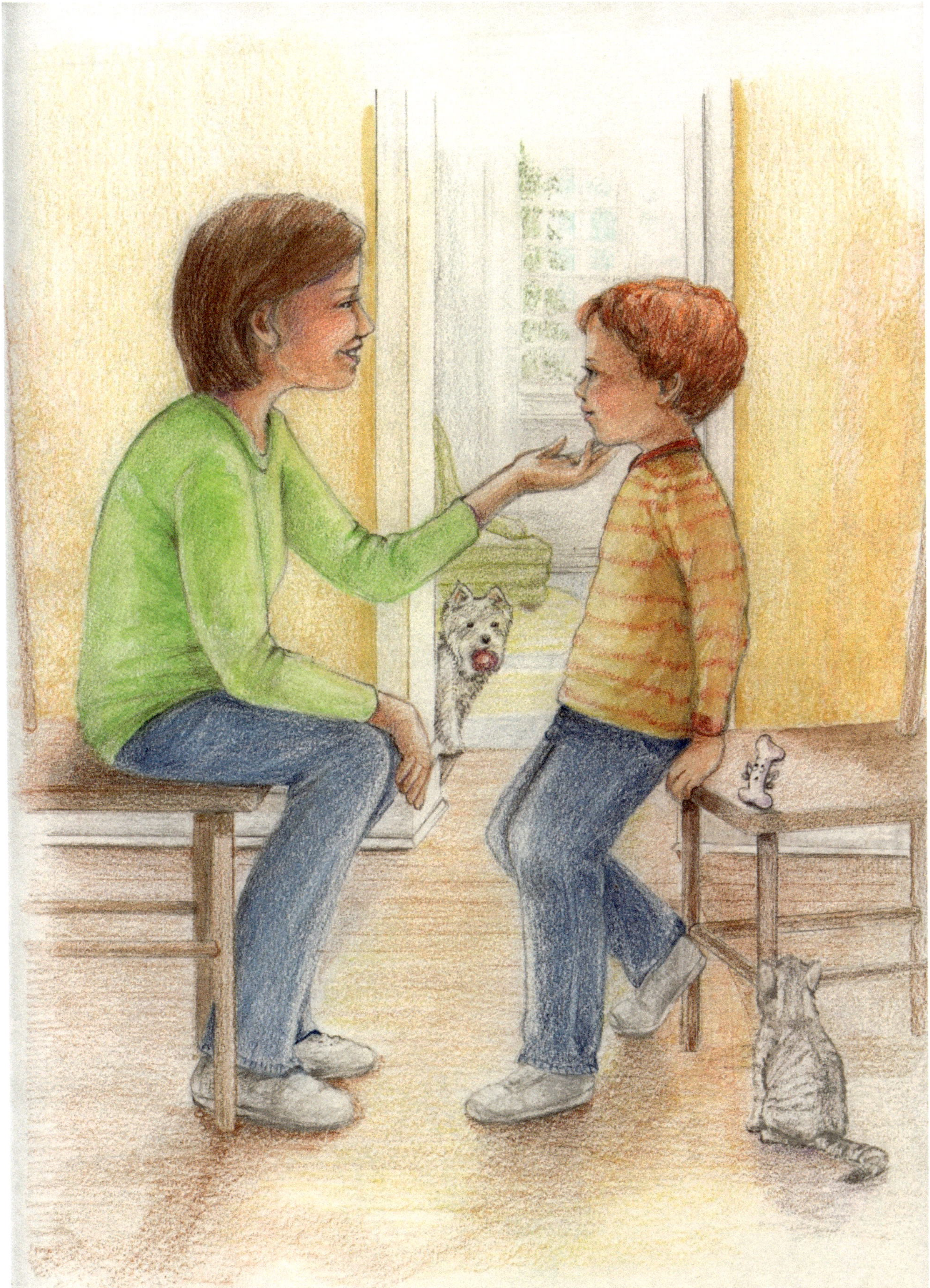

Mom and Eleanor watch as he tries to hold his elbow over his stomach like the moms in the park, but that doesn't make him laugh. He tries to throw his head back with his elbow on his forehead, but that doesn't make him laugh. He tries slapping his leg with his elbow but that doesn't make him laugh. It actually kind of hurts. Finally he tries holding his mouth and looking at his elbow thinking that maybe if he looks at his elbow he'll laugh, but he can't see his elbow.
"ARGH!" shouts Ellis: "It's not working!"

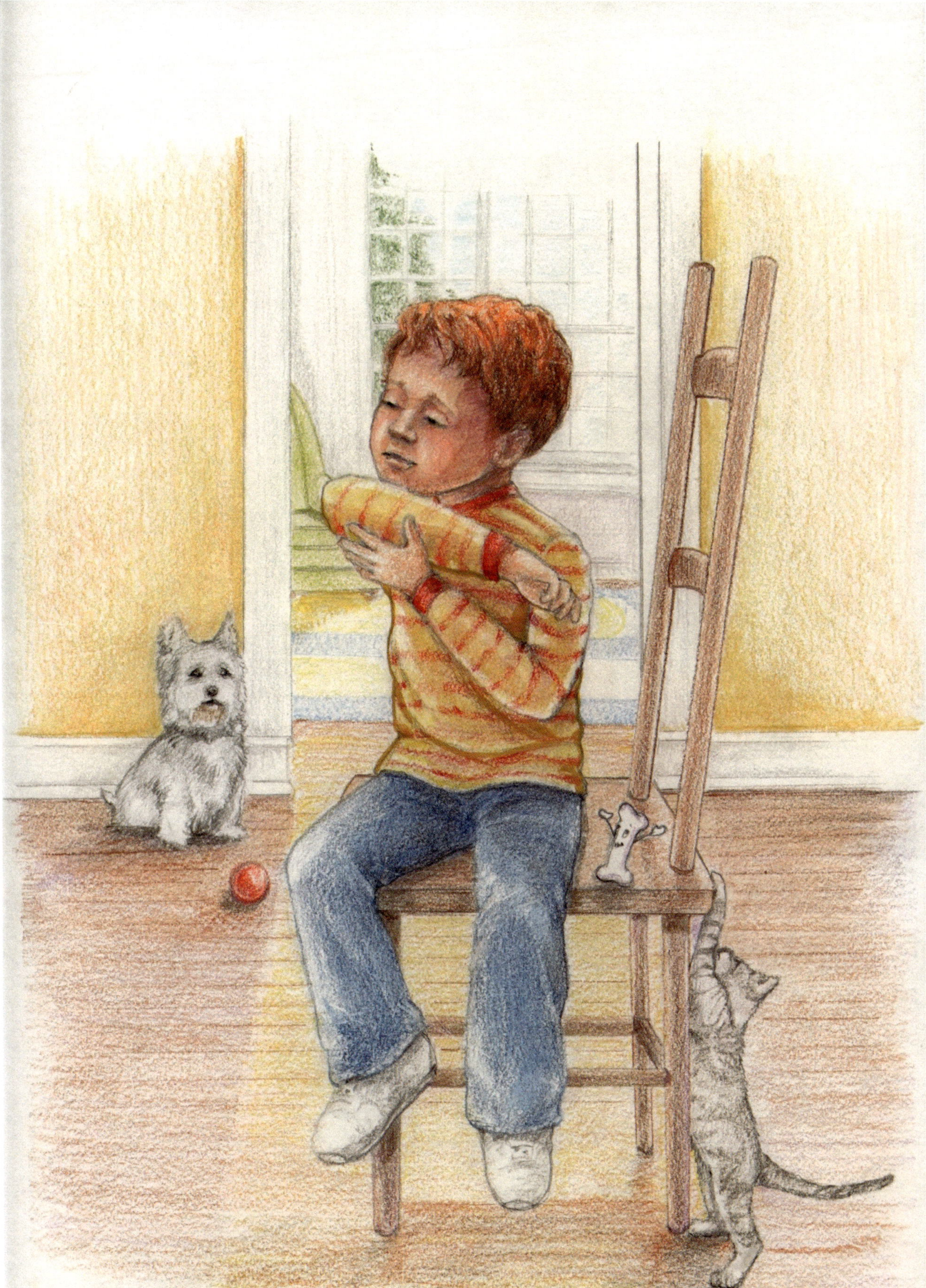

Mom smiles a little at first and then her smile grows. She explains, "Well, it's not like when you get tickled or when you're in a pillow fight and it's not funny like a joke. It only feels funny or strange when you accidentally hit your elbow on something. It gives you a funny, tingly feeling when it is injured or hurt. So it is called a funny bone. It is the only bone in your body that feels like that when you bump it."

Ellis thinks for a moment and stares at his Mom waiting for her to say something else. Ellis thinks his Mom is the smartest person in the whole world!

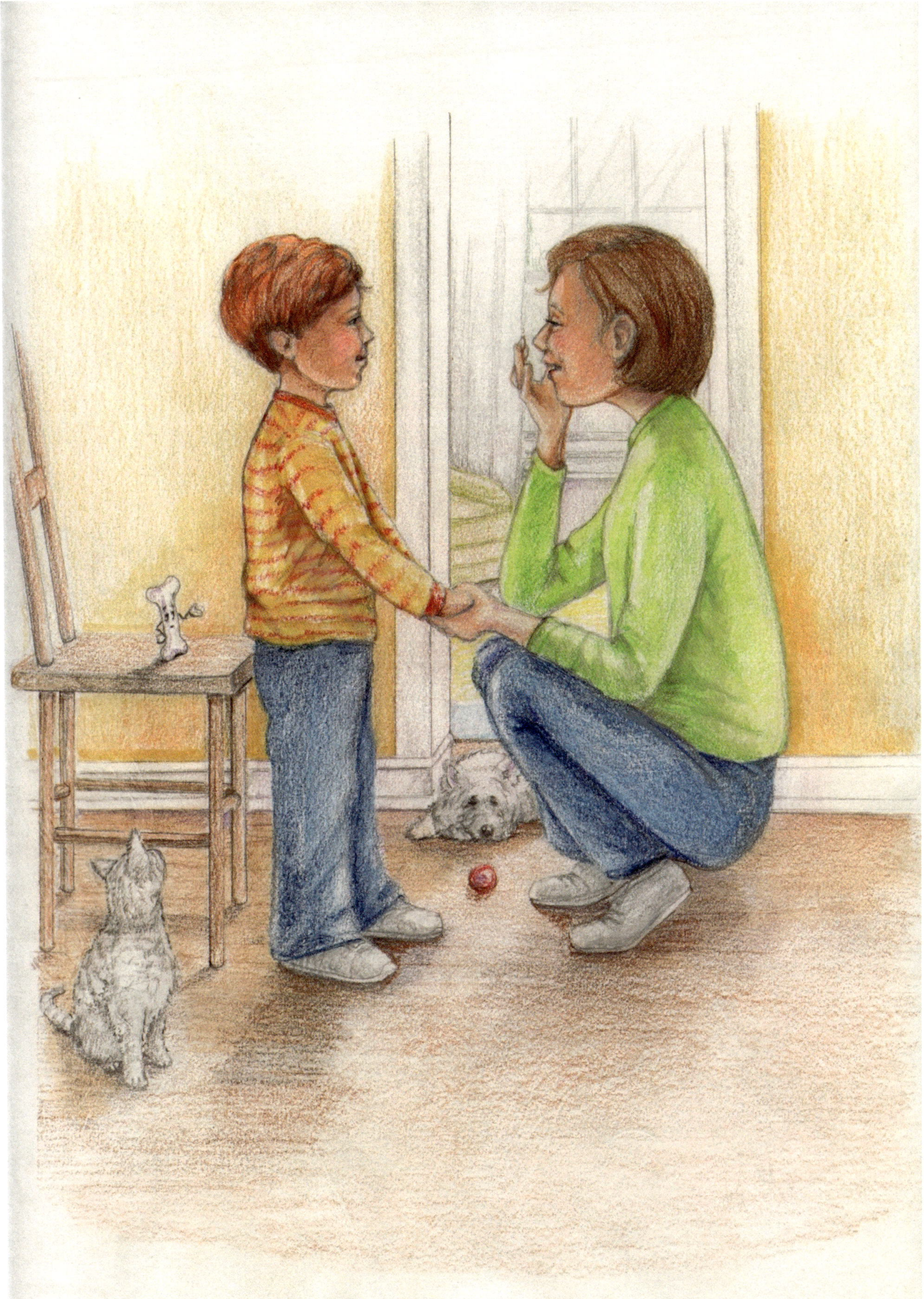

Ellis responds slowly with a scrunched up face, "Well....that's not funny!"

"No, I guess not," says Ellis' Mom with a smile.

She laughs again, covering her mouth. She looks at him and understands his confusion and slowly moves her hand away from her mouth revealing a bigger smile with lots of teeth.

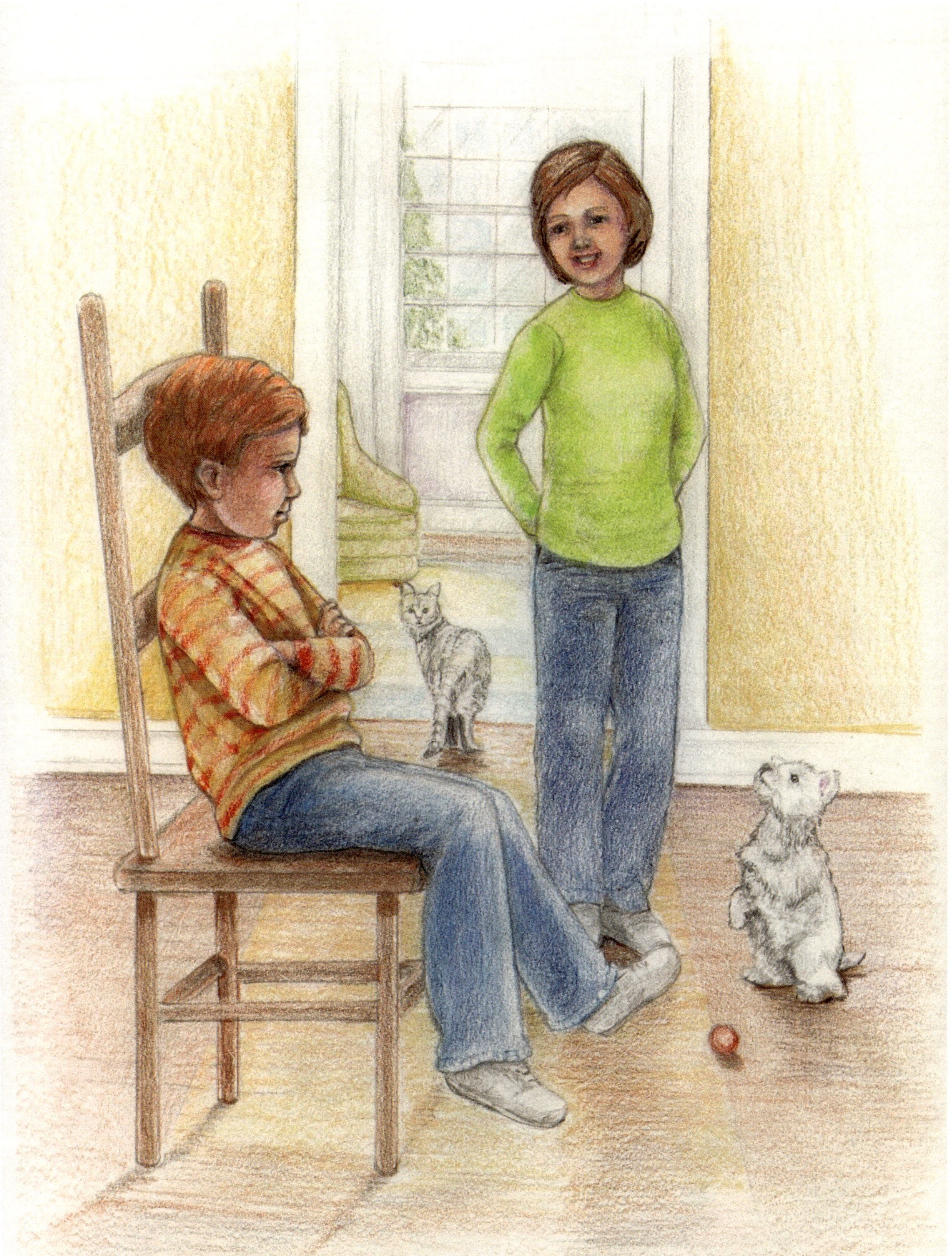

Ellis cannot help but look at her and smile back at her. Ellis thinks it would be a lot easier to understand if the funny bone was on the mouth because that's where smiles come from. Ellis smiles so that all of his teeth show and his Mom gives him a big hug.

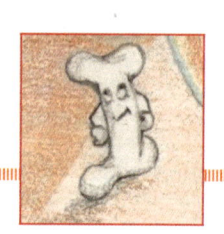

33

## Scientific explanation

The funny bone isn't a bone at all. It is a nerve called the **ulnar nerve** that goes along the inside part of your elbow. It controls the feeling in your fourth and fifth fingers and certain wrist movements, too! The **humerus** (hyoo-mer-us) is a long bone that starts at your shoulder and ends at your elbow. At the back of the elbow, the ulnar nerve is exposed (meaning that it doesn't have a lot of **muscles** or **ligaments** over it to protect it.) When this nerve is bumped or hit, it produces a tingling sensation. Some people describe this tingling as a "funny" sensation. Since it feels like a bone, it became known as the "funny bone." The funny bone is the only bone in your body that can't break!

# Anatomy of the Elbow

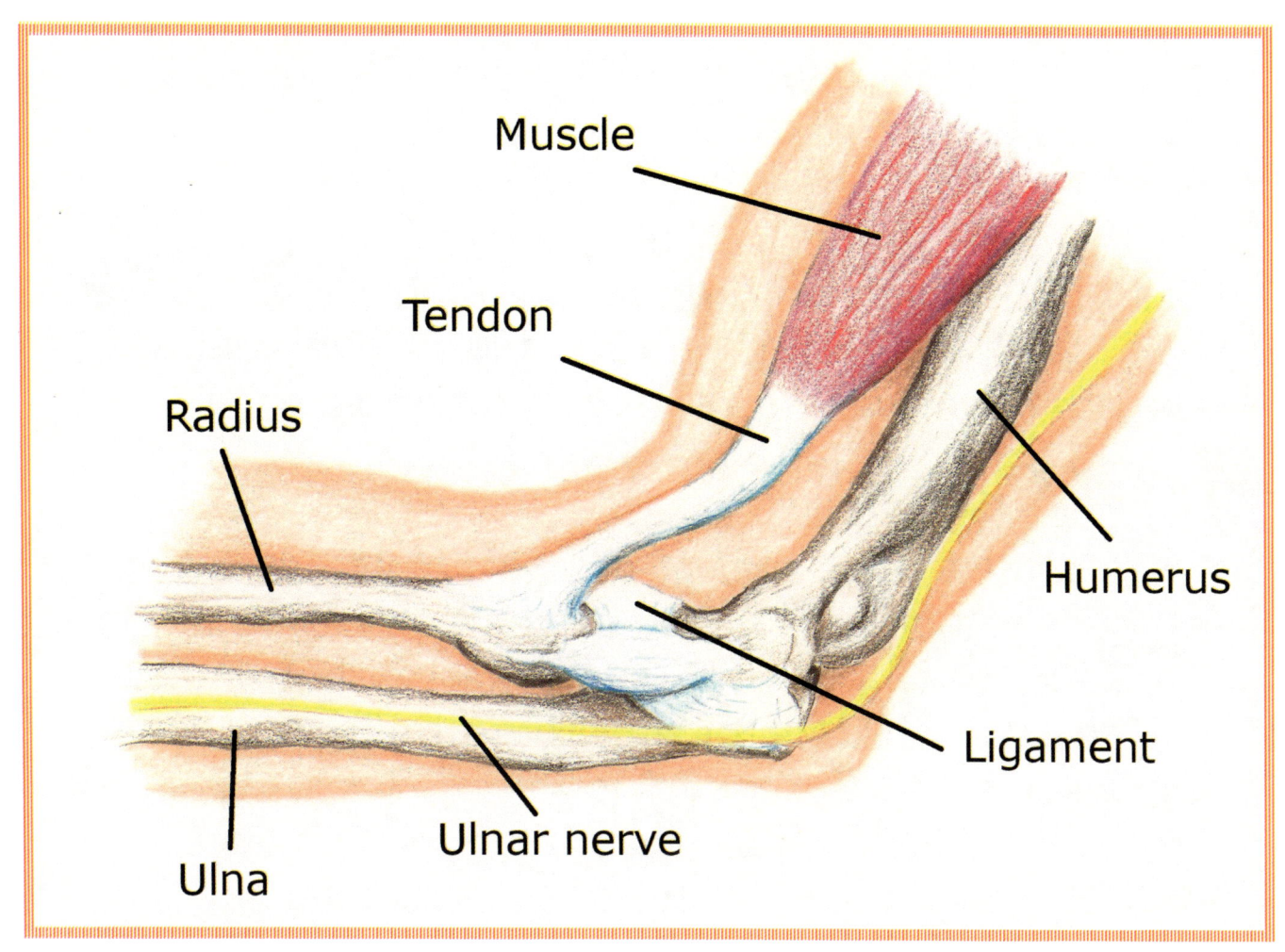

# Bone Facts

The adult human body has 206 bones. But an infant's body could have between 300 and 350 bones that will eventually fuse together to form 206 bones as a grown adult.

Of the 206 bones in the adult human body, more than half (106) are in the hands and feet. The adult skeleton consists of the following bones:
- 28 skull bones (8 cranial, 14 facial, and 6 ear bones)
- 1 bone in the front of the neck called the hyoid
- 26 vertebrae (7 neck; 12 thoracic; 5 lumbar; the sacrum, which is five fused vertebrae; and the coccyx, which is four fused vertebrae)
- 24 ribs and the breastbone;
- the shoulder (2 clavicles, and 2 scapulae)
- the pelvic bones (3 fused bones called the coxal bone or the hip girdle)
- 30 bones in each of the arms and legs (a total of 120 bones)
- a few partial bones, ranging from 8-18 bones which form joints.

## Etymology of the phrase "funny bone"

or where did the word phrase, "funny bone," come from?

Research shows that this phrase was first used in English language in the early 1800s. It became the nickname for the long bone in the arm that starts at the shoulder and ends at the elbow. The name of that bone is the Humerus (hyoo-mer-us), see illustration on page 36. Humerus and the word "humorous" sound almost the same. Humorous means funny so that's how this bone got its name.

# ABOUT THE INQUISITIVE ELLIS CONSTRUCTION TEAM

**Julianne Wells** graduated from West Chester University with a degree in English and was an editor with a publishing company where she met her husband, Brian. While raising her three boys, she went back to college and obtained a Masters of Education from Immaculata University and began teaching at the elementary level. It was in the classroom that she discovered the gap between the understanding of figurative verses literal language in the literature that she read to her students every day. Mrs. Wells was an educator for a dozen years in all elementary grade levels but enjoyed teaching the little people the most because they always asked the toughest questions.

**Fran Hughes** attended Philadelphia College of Art, then transferred to and graduated from Glassboro State College, now known as Rowan University, with a B.A. in Illustration. She began her college studies in the field of Education, but changed her major while her two sons attended high school to pursue a life-long love of art. Mrs. Hughes' work can be viewed at www.franhughesart.com.

**Dr. Michael J. Harkness** is a Wells family friend and was the pediatrician for the Wells boys. He is a graduate of St. Joseph University and the University of Pittsburgh. He completed his residency at the University of Alabama. Currently Dr. Harkness is the Chief of Outpatient Pediatrics at Main Line Health and has been a general pediatrician for 30 years.

**Sean Wells** is the second son of the author and is a graduate of the Savannah College of Art and Design. He is currently employed at Crozier Fine Arts. He paints for enjoyment and more of Sean's art can be viewed in his virtual gallery at www.scwellsdesigns.com.

Made in the USA
Charleston, SC
18 November 2015